JENNIFER DEAN

5 Minute Daily Devos for Kids

Solving the Mystery of the Fruit of the Spirit

This book was professionally typeset on Reedsy.
Find out more at reedsy.com

Contents

Introduction

Hey there, Detective Squad!

We're absolutely buzzing with excitement that you've decided to join us on this thrilling Bible quest to crack the case of the Fruit of the Spirit!

I'm Jen, and alongside my partner-in-crime (a.k.a. my son, Israel), we've whipped up this mini devotional just for you. It's a true delight and privilege to journey with you as we dive into God's Word over the next 14 days.

This devotional is like a supercharged snack for your spirit—just 5 minutes a day to squeeze into your routine! Our hope is that this time will refresh your soul, stir your heart, and pull you closer to God. Each day, we'll shine a spotlight on a specific fruit of the Spirit from Galatians 5:22-23 and dig into how to grow these juicy qualities in our lives.

Here's the fun stuff you can look forward to:

- Key Verse:We'll kick things off with a Bible verse that showcases the fruit of the Spirit we're zeroing in on for the day.
- Heart-to-Heart Sharing:Israel and I will spill some personal stories, lessons, and nuggets of encouragement to help you weave these

truths into your daily life.
- Scripture Memorization:Over the next two weeks, we'll also tackle memorizing Galatians 5:22-23 together. By the end, you'll have these powerful verses locked in your brain, ready to power up your walk with God!

We're so pumped for the surprises awaiting us during this time! So grab your Bible, cozy up in a quiet nook, and let's dive into God's Word together. We're sure these next 14 days will be a whirlwind of transformation, and we can't wait to see how God shakes things up in your life!

Let's solve this mystery together!

Day 1 - What's the Scoop on the Fruit of the Spirit?

Galatians 5:22-23

But the fruit of the Spirit is love, joy, peace, patience, kindness, goodness, faithfulness, gentleness, and self-control. Against such things, there is no law.

Welcome, detectives, to Day 1 of our divine detective adventure! Let's unravel the delicious mystery of what the fruit of the Spirit really is!

You'll find this juicy goodness nestled in Galatians 5:22-23. Over the next 14 days, we'll explore these verses, one scrumptious fruit at a time—like a spiritual scavenger hunt! Each fruit is like a sparkling gem reflecting God's character, ready to be discovered in our lives.

Imagine your heart as a fruit tree! When you tune in to God's frequency and follow His lead, your tree produces some seriously scrumptious, heavenly fruit. Each piece is a delightful treasure that lights up your life and puts a big smile on God's face.

Here's what your fruit tree can produce:

1. **Love** – Think of love as a plump, juicy strawberry, making you the ultimate bestie!

2. **Joy** – Joy is like a sunny, sweet orange, bursting with happiness, guaranteed to make you smile.

3. **Peace** – Picture peace as a soothing banana, keeping you cool as a cucumber when life gets bananas.

4. **Patience** – Patience is your pineapple pal, reminding you to chill out and wait it out like a pro.

5. **Kindness** – A soft, juicy peach that inspires you to sprinkle good deeds everywhere you go!

6. **Goodness** – Like a crunchy, delightful apple, goodness nudges you to do the right thing with a cheerful grin.

7. **Faithfulness** – A trusty grape, whispering sweet nothings about loyalty and keeping your promises.

8. **Gentleness** – Imagine a smooth, sweet pear, helping you be tender-hearted and gentle, spreading love like confetti.

9. **Self-control** – A refreshing watermelon, keeping you in check, reminding you to make those wise choices!

When we're plugged into Jesus, our tree overflows with this fantastic fruit, making us the ultimate blessing to everyone around us!

As we dive into these juicy qualities, we'll crack the case on why these fruits are essential for our hearts and lives. They'll help us strengthen our relationships, transform our attitudes, and guide our actions. By the end of these 14 days, we hope you'll not only understand these traits but also see them thriving in your life like never before!

Prayer:

Jesus, thank You for guiding us to uncover the mystery of the fruit of the Spirit. Over the next 14 days, help our hearts explode with Your amazing fruit! Amen.

Memorize:

Let's kick off this case with some memory magic by memorizing **Galatians 5:22-23** together! Feel free to bust out some dance moves or create fun pictures to help you remember these verses, just like we do!
"But the fruit of the Spirit is love, joy, peace,
patience, kindness, goodness, faithfulness,
gentleness, and self-control.
Against such things, there is no law."

Day 2 - The Scoop on the Fruit of Love

Galatians 5:22-23

But the fruit of the Spirit is **love**, joy, peace, patience, kindness, goodness, faithfulness, gentleness, and self-control. Against such things, there is no law.

Alright, detectives, it's time to unravel the juicy mystery of the fruit of love! We're diving deep into this topic over two days, starting now! So, what's love really all about? It's a head-scratcher for sure, but God's Word is here to help us crack this case wide open.

Let's talk about the ultimate Love: Jesus! Throughout His life, He showed love in every way imaginable—healing the sick, raising the dead, and the ultimate act of love: sacrificing Himself on the cross for us!

Seriously, how do we even sum up something as massive as love in just two devotionals? But here's the main takeaway: Jesus is the ultimate picture of love. He loves you and me to infinity and beyond, laying down His life so we can have a personal relationship with Him. That's love on a whole new level! When we grasp the depth of His love, we can't help but spread that love to everyone we meet. His love is flawless and never lets us down.

Isn't that amazing?!

Stay tuned as we continue to solve the mystery of His incredible love tomorrow!

Prayer:
Jesus, thank You for showing us what true love looks like! Help us soak in Your love and let it overflow from us every single day. Amen.

Memorize:
Let's learn these verses to a catchy tune! Check out YouTube or Spotify (with your parents' permission, of course) for some fun Fruit of the Spirit songs. One of our faves comes from Slugs and Bugs!
Galatians 5:22-23
"But the fruit of the Spirit is love, joy, peace,
patience, kindness, goodness, faithfulness,
gentleness, and self-control.
Against such things, there is no law."

Day 3 - The Scoop on Love Part Two

Galatians 5:22-23

But the fruit of the Spirit is **love**, joy, peace, patience, kindness, goodness, faithfulness, gentleness, and self-control. Against such things, there is no law.

Alright, detectives, let's dive deeper! Now that we learned that Jesus is the ultimate example of Love, how do we reflect that love to others as the fruit of the Spirit?

We're so glad you asked!

Let's unwrap some super famous love verses from 1 Corinthians 13:4-8: "Love is patient, love is kind. It does not envy, it does not boast, it is not proud. 5 It does not dishonour others, it is not self-seeking, it is not easily angered, it keeps no record of wrongs. 6 Love does not delight in evil but rejoices with the truth. 7 It always protects, always trusts, always hopes, always perseveres. 8 Love never fails."

Whoa, that's a treasure chest of wisdom, team! And guess what? Some of those love descriptors are also part of the Spiritual fruit salad we're learning about! It's all woven together like a divine tapestry!

Living out love means we mirror Jesus in everything we do:

When our siblings are being total goofballs, we forgive them.

When someone stomps on our feelings, we keep calm and carry on.

When a friend pulls a betrayal stunt, we don't stoop to their level.

Love never fails!

Let's be the kind of kids that shine Jesus' love like a bright beacon, no matter the storm!

Prayer:
Jesus, thank You for cracking open the mystery of true love and showing us how to love and be loved. Help us beam Your spectacular love to our siblings, friends, and neighbours every day (even on the tough days!). Amen.

Memorize:
Time to turn our memory skills up to detective level, pals! Let's say Galatians 5:22-23 together:
Galatians 5:22-23
"But the fruit of the Spirit is love, joy, peace,
patience, kindness, goodness, faithfulness,
gentleness, and self-control.
Against such things, there is no law."

Day 4 - The Scoop on The Fruit of Joy

Galatians 5:22-23

But the fruit of the Spirit is love, *joy*, peace, patience, kindness, goodness, faithfulness, gentleness and self-control. Against such things there is no law.

Alright, take a moment to flash your brightest, snazziest smile in the mirror! Now, imagine that dazzling smile lighting up someone else's day. Smiles and laughter are the sprinkles on the joy sundae, but let's dig deeper, detectives!

Joy is like discovering that God loves us SO much He sent His only Son (Jesus) so that anyone who believes in Him gets eternal life! Whoa! That's the root of our joy, friends! Knowing we have a personal relationship with the Creator of theUniverse Who genuinely cares for us. This joy is like the ultimate treasure, way deeper than any shiny new toy, scrumptious ice cream cone, or thrilling vacation (though those are pretty sweet too!). It's a heart-fueled joy that doesn't depend on what's happening around us—way more reliable than a good laugh or a blockbuster comedy. This kind of happiness helps us keep on truckin', no matter what life tosses our way!

As we focus on Jesus and His goodness, we can bubble over with joy every single day! Your smile will shine brighter than ever as you soak in just how much He cares for you.

That's the scoop on joy in a nutshell!

Prayer:
Jesus, thanks for the fruit of joy and that it's rooted in our awesome relationship with You. Help us blossom in joy as we discover just how much You love and care for us in countless ways. Let us shine with joy! Amen.

Memorize:
Have you jammed out to a song about the fruit of the Spirit? Let's belt it out together!
Galatians 5:22-23
"But the fruit of the Spirit is love, joy, peace,
patience, kindness, goodness, faithfulness,
gentleness, and self-control.
Against such things there is no law."

Day 5 - The Scoop on The Fruit of Peace

Galatians 5:22-23

But the fruit of the Spirit is love, joy, **peace**, patience, kindness, goodness, faithfulness, gentleness and self-control. Against such things there is no law.

Ever found yourself knee-deep in stress? Stuck in a traffic jam that feels like a lifetime? Or maybe you've felt a heart-wrenching sadness that hits you right in the feels? Oh, I've been there too! Sometimes, in that sea of sadness and the whirlwind of life, anxiety sneaks in like an uninvited guest. It can feel like a heavy blanket smothering you, almost paralyzing. But fear not, my peace-seeking pals, because here comes the Spirit of Peace to save the day!

Let's do something together - let's take a nice, slow, deep breath. Ahhhhhhhh. Inhale… exhale. Sigh.

Isn't that just the bee's knees? That long, deep breath is like a mini-vacation for your soul! That's what peace feels like: a warm hug assuring you that everything will be alright. Why? Not because life is always a walk in the park, but because we know the ultimate superhero—God! He's got every little detail of our lives in His capable hands, and His Word promises that He makes all things work together for good for those who love Him and are on His mission. (Romans 8:28)

Peace comes from knowing the Prince of Peace, Jesus Himself.

Let's take a moment to soak that in and breathe deep. He is more than enough!

Prayer:
Jesus, thank You for being the Prince of Peace! As we dig our roots deeper into our relationship with You, spending time in prayer and getting to know You, we can embrace peace every single day. Amen.

Memorize:
Alright, detectives, let's flex those brain muscles and recite Galatians 5:22-23 together:
Galatians 5:22-23
"But the fruit of the Spirit is love, joy, peace,
patience, kindness, goodness, faithfulness,
gentleness, and self-control.
Against such things there is no law."

Day 6 - The Scoop on the Fruit of Patience

Galatians 5:22-23

But the fruit of the Spirit is love, joy, peace, **patience**, kindness, goodness, faithfulness, gentleness and self-control. Against such things there is no law.

As a kiddo, my twin brother and I loved jamming to this hilarious tune called "Patience." It had this catchy line: "I can't wait to have patience, because patience is a wonderful thing. Hurry up, let me have it, gotta have it now…I want it more than anything. This has taken long enough, give me some of that patience stuff!"

It cracked us up because it perfectly captured our struggle with wanting patience right this second! But guess what? Cultivating that sweet fruit of patience is a marathon, not a sprint. The sneaky thing about patience is that it often grows when we're stuck in those waiting rooms of life.

Like waiting for Christmas in July, standing in a line that feels like a lifetime at the amusement park, or saving every penny for that epic gift for our sibling. Patience means keeping our lips zipped and trusting that God has a master plan with impeccable timing.

Sure, patience isn't the fastest fruit to ripen, but as we lean into our trust in God, that delightful fruit will turn us into the kind of friends everyone wants to hang out with during life's waiting game.

Prayer:
Jesus, thanks for reminding us that in the waiting, You're cooking up something good for us and those around us. Help us rock that patience, no matter what life throws our way. Amen.

Memorize:
Alright, memory champions, let's sharpen those recall skills:
Galatians 5:22-23
"But the fruit of the Spirit is love, joy, peace,
patience, kindness, goodness, faithfulness,
gentleness and self-control.
Against such things there is no law."

Day 7 - The Scoop on The Fruit of Kindness

Galatians 5:22-23

But the fruit of the Spirit is love, joy, peace, patience, **kindness**, goodness, faithfulness, gentleness and self-control. Against such things there is no law.

Ah, kindness! That buzzword we can't escape these days. "Be kind!" they say. It's super easy, yet packs a mighty punch! Kindness is simply being nice to those around us—unless they're being total grumps, then it gets tricky! That's when we need the Holy Spirit's help to enable us to be kind even on our grumpiest days.

The ultimate kindness star? Jesus! He showed us how to sprinkle kindness everywhere, even to those who might not deserve it (yikes!). He taught us to pray for our foes and treat everyone with love. Talk about a kindness masterclass!

So, how about we play detective over the next couple of days and dive into some Jesus stories? Let's unravel the mystery of kindness together!

And tomorrow, we'll crack open the mystery of kindness even wider!

Prayer:
Jesus, you are the ultimate kindness champion! Help us learn more about You and let kindness burst from us like a fountain every single day! Amen.

Memorize:
Today's mission: write down our Bible memory verses!
Galatians 5:22-23
"But the fruit of the Spirit is love,
joy, peace, patience, kindness,
goodness, faithfulness, gentleness, and self-control.
Against such things there is no law."

Day 8 - The Scoop on the Fruit of Kindness Part Two

Galatians 5:22-23

But the fruit of the Spirit is love, joy, peace, patience, **kindness**, goodness, faithfulness, gentleness and self-control. Against such things there is no law.

Alright, team! Gather 'round because today we're diving into some super sleuthing to uncover the mystery of the Fruit of Kindness! Are you pumped?

Let's put on our thinking caps and brainstorm all the delightful ways to sprinkle kindness on everyone—siblings, parents, grandparents, neighbours and friends! Don't forget to team up with your family for some brainstorming fun!

Some ideas are as easy as sharing some food with your neighbours, gifting your sibling that must-have toy they've been eyeing, or inviting that lonely friend to join your game.

Once you've cooked up a list of kindness ideas, it's time to roll up those sleeves and put them into action! For the next week, we challenge you to pull off one act of kindness every single day.

Let's make kindness the coolest daily habit, so even on those grumpy days, we can still share the sweetness of kindness with everyone we meet.

Off we go, detectives!

P.S. We want to hear all about your amazing acts of kindness! Shoot us an email or find us on social media to share your adventures (with your parents' thumbs up, of course).

Prayer:
Jesus, help us spread Your kindness everywhere, especially in our own homes. Thanks for the wisdom and ideas to keep kindness alive every day. Amen.

Memorize:
Let's do it, detectives! Join me in saying:
Galatians 5:22-23
"But the fruit of the Spirit is love, joy, peace,
patience, kindness, goodness, faithfulness,
gentleness and self-control.
Against such things there is no law."

Day 9 - The Scoop on the Fruit of Goodness

Galatians 5:22-23

But the fruit of the Spirit is love, joy, peace, patience, kindness, **goodness**, faithfulness, gentleness and self-control. Against such things there is no law.

Hey there, friends! Today we're diving into the delightful world of goodness! Think of it as simply doing what's right—easy-peasy, right? But hold up! What happens when the goodness train derails because someone else isn't playing nice? Or when you're stuck between a rock and a hard place, trying to choose between honesty and a little white lie—especially when the truth could land you in hot water?

That's when we need our secret weapon—the Holy Spirit—to boost our detective skills and help us make the right call, even when it feels like climbing a mountain or when it costs us a little something. Goodness is all about showing kindness and love, even when it feels like we're giving a hug to a cactus. It's about sharing that shiny toy when all we want to do is sprint away with it, or letting someone snag a bite of our delicious treat when our inner self just wants to hoard it all!

That's the juicy fruit of goodness, my fellow detectives! It might not always be a walk in the park, but trust me, it's totally worth it in the end!

Prayer:
Jesus, thanks a million for showering us with goodness every single day—from the sunny skies to blooming flowers, tasty treats, and a loving family. We're so grateful for Your goodness, and we ask for help in spreading that goodness to everyone we meet. Amen.

Memorize:
How's that memorization coming along, detectives? Keep up the awesome work! If you're hitting a snag, just revisit that catchy song about the fruit of the Spirit—it's a total lifesaver!
Galatians 5:22-23
"But the fruit of the Spirit is love, joy, peace,
patience, kindness, goodness, faithfulness,
gentleness and self-control.
Against such things there is no law."

Day 10- The Scoop on the Fruit of Faithfulness

Galatians 5:22-23

But the fruit of the Spirit is love, joy, peace, patience, kindness, goodness, **faithfulness**, gentleness and self-control. Against such things there is no law.

Good day, sleuths! Welcome to the thrilling day 10 of our fruit-filled investigation! You're absolutely nailing it!

Today's juicy target is the fruit of faithfulness! Faithfulness means standing your ground in the quest to follow Jesus, come rain or shine. It's about being the ultimate loyal buddy and sticking to your promises. And yes, it's also about being that amazing friend, even when they're not looking!

Sticking with Jesus can be a bit of a tightrope walk, especially when your fam or pals aren't on the same page. But trust me, He's the real deal worth rooting for! Just like being a loyal sibling or friend is the bee's knees, being a dedicated follower of Jesus takes the cake! Why? Because His faithfulness is like a never-ending party of love that never lets us down!

So let's put on our detective hats and be the loyal sidekicks who stick to our guns no matter what!

Prayer:
Jesus, thank You for being our forever, faithful friend. You never bail on us or let us down. Help us to be just as faithful to You and to be the best pals we can be. With You, we can tackle anything! Amen.

Memorize:
Let's join forces and whisper our memory verses together today!
Galatians 5:22-23
"But the fruit of the Spirit is love, joy, peace,
patience, kindness, goodness, faithfulness,
gentleness and self-control.
Against such things there is no law."

Day 11- The Scoop on the Fruit of Gentleness

Galatians 5:22-23

But the fruit of the Spirit is love, joy, peace, patience, kindness, goodness, faithfulness, **gentleness** and self-control. Against such things there is no law.

Did you know the New Testament was originally penned in Greek? Yep, it's true! The Greek word for "gentleness" in Galatians 5 actually translates to humility. So, what's the scoop on being humble and gentle?

Gentleness can be a slippery little fruit to define! In the New Testament, it paints a picture of someone who serves others with genuine humility and a boatload of patience. It's like letting God take the wheel and shape your character each day.

Now, friends, when we bask in the incredible, unconditional love of Jesus, we realize just how much we've got to be grateful for! That gratitude opens the floodgates, allowing us to share our treasure with others, including that sweet fruit of gentleness. With our hearts set on Jesus, being gentle to those who throw shade at us becomes just a tad easier.

So let's sprinkle a little gentleness and humility on our siblings, parents, and neighbours every single day. We can do it with the power of the Holy Spirit!

Prayer:
Jesus, You are the ultimate gentle giant! Even when life threw You massive trials, You chose humility. You trusted God's plan, even when it was tough. Please help us to do the same! Amen.

Memorize:
Whip out that page where you jotted down Galatians 5:22-23, and let's dive into it together!
Galatians 5:22-23
"But the fruit of the Spirit is love, joy, peace,
patience, kindness, goodness, faithfulness,
gentleness and self-control.
Against such things there is no law."

Day 12- The Scoop on the Fruit of Self Control

Galatians 5:22-23

But the fruit of the Spirit is love, joy, peace, patience, kindness, goodness, faithfulness, gentleness and ***self-control***. Against such things there is no law.

Alright, detectives, we've reached the grand finale of our Spiritual fruit lineup—self-control! Bravo for making it this far! Oh boy, what a doozy to wrap things up with!

So, what's the scoop on self-control? It's a compound word smoothie made from "self" and "control." We all know what "self" is, but when we toss in "control," we're diving into the deep end! Ever felt like bursting with excitement in a library, only to unleash a loud squeal? Fun times, but oops, wrong venue! Or maybe you've had a spat with a sibling and let your tongue run wild instead of biting it? Or indulged on sweets until your tummy was questioning your life choices?

That, my friends, is where self-control swoops in like a superhero! We need the Holy Spirit to help us flex those self-control muscles in every nook and cranny of our lives—whether it's on the school playground, in Sunday school, or shushing in the library.

Jesus was the ultimate example of self-control, turning down temptation like a pro. Instead of giving in to what was easy, He chose the righteous path and shouted "No!" to the wrong stuff. And guess what? We can do it too—with a little help from our Divine buddy, the Holy Spirit, every single day!

We're totally capable of this with His help!

Prayer:
Jesus, You showed us how to say no to temptation and rock that self-control! Help me follow Your lead with all my heart, soul, mind, and strength every single day. Amen!

Memorize:
Now let's get ready to shout out our Bible verses! (Close your eyes and let's go!)
Galatians 5:22-23
"But the fruit of the Spirit is love, joy, peace,
patience, kindness, goodness, faithfulness,
gentleness and self-control.
Against such things there is no law."

Day 13 - The Scoop on "No Law"

Galatians 5:22-23

But the fruit of the Spirit is love, joy, peace, patience, kindness, goodness, faithfulness, gentleness and self-control. Against such things there is **no law**.

Friends, buckle up because our final batch of verses may feel like a riddle wrapped in a mystery inside an enigma! So, what's the scoop when Paul (the guy who wrote Galatians) drops the line "against such things there is no law"?

Earlier in the book of Galatians, Paul was dishing out some juicy tidbits about freedom in Christ. When we strut our stuff living out the fruit of the Spirit daily, we're totally agreeing with God's flawless law—His ultimate game plan for our lives. That's why there's no "law" against the fruit of the Spirit; it's all sunshine and rainbows when you live this way! But let's be real—none of us nail it perfectly every single day, no matter how hard we flex. Why? Because we're human, and we trip and tumble!

Here's the cherry on top: when we chase after Jesus with our whole hearts, souls, minds, and strength, each day turns sweeter than the last, and eventually the fruit of our lives becomes a delicious banquet!

Prayer:
Holy Spirit, thank You for living in us and helping us bloom with good fruit every day. Help us spread Your goodness to our families, friends, and neighbours so that Your love shines bright to everyone we meet. Amen.

Memorize:
As we wrap up our last two devotionals together, let's challenge ourselves to recite our verses from memory—let's go for gold!
Galatians 5:22-23
"But the fruit of the Spirit is love, joy, peace,
patience, kindness, goodness, faithfulness,
gentleness and self-control.
Against such things there is no law."

Day 14 - The Scoop on LIVING It

Galatians 5:22-23

But the fruit of the Spirit is love, joy, peace, patience, kindness, goodness, faithfulness, gentleness and self-control. Against such things there is no law.

Hey there, Detective Squad! You've totally crushed it over the past 14 days! We're bursting with excitement as you've walked hand-in-hand with us learning about the fruit of the Spirit and deepened your bond with Jesus Christ!

Now, let's wrap up our time together by chatting about how we can sprinkle that Spiritual fruit into our daily grind. Let's face it, life can feel like a rollercoaster with ups and downs! So, how do we stay plugged into the Vine—aka Jesus—and keep producing that delicious fruit we've been exploring?

The secret sauce? Leaning into your relationship with Jesus every single day—just like you've been doing! Dive into the Bible, memorize verses, and live them out. Finding a vibrant Church crew who's all about loving Jesus is also a game-changer. Keep that line of communication open with Jesus, reaching out to Him in every moment to tap into our Ultimate Source of wisdom, strength, and love. And don't forget to spread the joy by showing love, joy, peace, patience, kindness, goodness, faithfulness, gentleness, and self-control to your family, friends, and neighbours. How? Easy peasy! Just sprinkle in simple acts of kindness every day!

Hold the door for someone.
Flash a smile at a friend.
Share some treats with the neighbours.
Rake leaves for an elderly neighbour.
Mow the lawn for someone who can't.

Keep pouring out the love you've received from Jesus and watch your life's fruit grow sweeter by the day!

We're super proud of you, friends!

Prayer:
Jesus, thank You for showing us how to live a life bursting with this delightful fruit. Help us reflect Your love to everyone we meet—especially at home. Amen.

Memorize:
One last shout-out (and let's live it out!):
Galatians 5:22-23
"But the fruit of the Spirit is love, joy, peace,
patience, kindness, goodness, faithfulness,

gentleness and self-control.
Against such things there is no law."

If you've loved this Bible study, keep your eyes peeled for more fun stuff coming your way soon!

HUGE Blessings!

Israel & Jen

9 781069 080103